Scandinavian-American Genealogical Resources

Dr. Charles Dickson

HERITAGE BOOKS
2007

HERITAGE BOOKS
AN IMPRINT OF HERITAGE BOOKS, INC.

Books, CDs, and more—Worldwide

For our listing of thousands of titles see our website
at
www.HeritageBooks.com

Published 2007 by
HERITAGE BOOKS, INC.
Publishing Division
65 East Main Street
Westminster, Maryland 21157-5026

International Standard Book Number: 978-0-7884-1810-5

THE AUTHOR

Dr. Dickson is a college chemistry instructor and an ordained minister in addition to being a freelance writer. He holds degrees from the University of Tampa, Wartburg Theological Seminary, Stetson University, and the University of Florida.

He has authored books in both religion and chemistry and his historical articles have appeared in Scandinavian Review, The American Dane, The finnish American Newsletter, Genealogical Helper, Heritage Quest, and Ancestry Newsletter.

He is a Swedish-American whose grandparents came to Jamestown, New York from Vimmerby in the Småland area of Sweden in the 1870s. This book is the result of his lifelong interest in Scandinavian-American culture.

PREFACE

When Leif Ericsson touched the shores of Newfoundland around the year 1000, the Scandinavian-American story began. But another seven centuries would pass before the Scandinavian presence in the new world would take root.

The following pages represent an attempt to trace the history of this millennial saga by identifying sources of family records for each of the five individual Nordic groups (Danish, Finnish, Icelandic, Norwegian, and Swedish) plus some resources that have documents for all the groups.

In addition to repositories that are national in scope some local libraries and regional historical societies with information on specific groups are listed, plus a bibliography.

It is the hope of the writer that this work will serve as a tool to stimulate further interest in genealogical research.

Hickory, North Carolina   CD

TABLE OF CONTENTS

FINDING ANCESTORS IN AMERICA

Back when Alex Haley's book and television series titled <u>Roots</u> appeared, there was a great new interest sparked among Americans to learn more about their backgrounds. Societies desiring to help us in our search for ancestors began popping up like dandelions in the springtime. We all want to know more about our ancestors, but how do we go about doing this?

Of course, some people hope to make exciting discoveries like finding out they are related to famous people, but most just want to know more about their grandparents or great-grandparents who first came to American shores.

Searching for your roots can be a very exciting journey. It may take you through old cemeteries, courthouses, libraries, houses of worship and homes of relatives just to mention a few. While doing this you may also learn a lot about history, geography, language, law, and religion as well as learning about your great Aunt Wilhelmina or great Uncle Oscar. To begin the trip you don't need a lot of tools, spades, fishing tackles, or horses --- all you need is a good notebook, an inquisitive mind, and a lot of imagination.

The first step in taking any trip is to map out the places through which you will pass. That is equally true for the trip in tracing your roots. In my own research I have found some definite steps to be helpful in turning up long-lost ancestors. Here's the plan:

1. Begin by talking to your relatives. Their memories and family records can be a good starting point. Of course you must be aware that their memories can be faulty or inaccurate at times, but this will at least provide a foundation for further investigation.

2. Don't forget friends of your relatives. They may add valuable extra points to your information which relatives forgot.

3. Check written records of family histories including items like old diaries and family Bibles. Diaries often produce interesting anecdotes concerning ancestors --- some of which you'd like to forget and others of which you'd like to brag about to your friends.

4. Search court records and notary publics. They are excellent sources, usually quite complete and admittedly more reliable than Granny's diary.

5. Places of business may provide you with insight into the type of work your ancestors were engaged in.

6. There are some great national genealogical collections especially if you have access to the metropolitan libraries in Boston, New York, Chicago, and Los Angeles. The Library of Congress collection is outstanding and the Church of Jesus Christ of Latter Day Saints in Salt Lake City is the largest records depository in the United States.

7. If the above are not available to you, don't overlook family records of local history that are maintained by many town libraries.

8. If you know the church or synagogue to which your ancestors belonged, they often have long-standing records of births, baptisms, weddings, and funerals.

9. Most major American religious groups have national depositories with valuable information. I discovered some of my own Swedish Lutheran records in the Augustana archives in Rock Island, Illinois.

10. America is a fabric composed of many ethnic strands. A number of historical societies have been established by various nationalities.

HAPPY HUNTING!

FINDING ANCESTORS IN DENMARK

The genealogical researcher should be aware that all of the Scandinavian countries, had a patronymic naming system until about 1860. For example, the son of a man named Anders would be called Andersen or Anderson and his daughter would be Andersdottir. Permanent surnames were established in Denmark between 1771 (in the south) and 1828 (in the north). Many people continued to use patronymics, but usually a church entry contained both names.

Having said this we now move to the particulars of the search for ancestors in Denmark.

In 1970 the number of counties in Denmark was reduced and many changed their names. The new counties are Aarhus, Bornholm, Frederiksborg, Fyn, Københavns, Nordjylland, Ribe, Ringkøbing, Roskilde, Randers, Sonderjylland, Storstrøm, Vejle, Viborg, and Vestjaelland.

The following information on location of archives and records in Denmark is provided by Angus Baxter's book <u>In Search of Your European Roots: A Complete Guide to Tracing Your Ancestors in Every Country in Europe</u>.

The National Archives are located at Rigsdagsgården 9, 1218 Copenhagen K. However, the main sources of genealogical information are in the four state archives known as Landsarkiver:
1. Landsarkivet for Sjaelland, Jagtvej 10, 2200 Copenhagen N
2. Landsarkivet for Fyn, Jernbanegade 36, 5000 Odense
3. Landsarkivet for Nørrejylland, Hansgade 5, 8800 Viborg
4. Landsarkivet for de Sønderjyske Lansdele, Haderslevvej 45, 6200 Aabenraa

Civil registration. While the Lutheran Church, which is the state church, is responsible for records of births, marriages, deaths, etc., there are some civil records outside the church. These include:

1. Civil registration of births, marriages, and deaths for the counties of Aabenraa-Sønderborg, Haderslev, and Tonder exist from 1874 and are in the state archives at Aabenraa.

2. Death certificates for the districts of Zealand, Fyn, Bornholm, and Lolland-Falster from 1857 are in the state archives at Copenhagen.

3. Some civil marriages were recorded from 1851 and these can be found in state or city archives.

4. Records of marriage licenses for the city of Copenhagen (1735-1868) are in the city archives at Copenhagen.

It should be noted that a major problem of ancestor hunting in Denmark is the duplication of personal names and place-names. For example, there are 114 places in Denmark named Skovlund. Your search for ancestors should include the following:

1. Church Registers. These include the Lutheran, Roman Catholic, the Reformed Churches, Episcopal, Methodist, and Jewish communities. All church records of every denomination up to 1891 are located in the state archives covering the particular district. Since 1891, a copy of the parish register has been sent to the state archives thirty years after it has been completed. Before 1814 marriage registers included only the names of the bride and groom, but since that time also include date and place of birth.

2. Betrothal. These are the equivalent of banns of other churches and may contain valuable information.

3. Confirmation. From 1736 most parishes recorded conformations, and after 1814 it was customary to list the names of the parents.

4. Introduction. After each child was born, the mother was regarded as being "unclean". Then after a period of two weeks she was regarded as cleansed and introduced to the congregation. Many dates are recorded.

5. Communion. These records date back to 1645 and usually include name and address.

6. Absolution. These records started in the mid 1600s and were discontinued in 1767. They give names of the persons and often details of the transgression.

7. Vaccination. They started in 1800 and are now found in confirmation of marriage records.

8. Lutheran Parish Register Extracts. These cover the period between the 17th and 19th centuries and are usually confined to nobility

9. Arrival Lists. From 1814 to 1875, the minister was required to record arrivals and departures from the parish. This law was primarily enforced in rural areas.

10. Removal Lists. Much the same as above, but also included the parish to which the person was moving.

11. General Schematic Registers. These were supposed to include names of everyone in the parish. Some parishes have kept better records than others.

12. Police Census. These cover the period from 1869 to 1923 dealing primarily with the residents of Copenhagen.

13. Censuses. Some of these go back to 1787. Check with municipal archives in areas where you are doing research.

14. Emigration. These records were kept from 1868 to 1959 and are in Landsarkivet Sjaelland.

15. Passport Records. These may be found in the various Landsarkiver for the period 1780-1920.

16. Marriage Licenses. These are for the city of Copenhagen for 1720-1868 only and are in the city archives.

17. Army Services. These records are in the Haerens Arkiv, Copenhagen, and some Navy records from 1802 are in the National Archives.

18. Deeds and Mortgages. These date from 1580 and contain names and addresses of contracting parties and description of properties.

19. Trade Guilds. The National Archives is the best place for these records although some smaller towns and guilds also have records.

20. Servants. These records were kept from 1828-1923 and are in the state archives.

21. Trade Licenses. These are found in the state archives and list the particular businesses and occupations.

22. Schools. These records are either in the state archives or in the original schools and go back to 1584.

23. Probate Records. These records go back to the 14th century and are located in the state archives.

24. Court Records. These records are in the National Archives as well as state archives and contain much legal information.

25. Genealogical Organizations. There are two of these including the Sanfundet for Dansk Genealogi or Personal-historie located at Crysgaardsvej 2, 2400 Copenhagen which maintains records but does not do research, and the Det Danske Udvandrerarkiv at v/Vor Frue Kirk P.O. Box 731 9100 Aalborg which is ready to assist Americans of Danish extraction.

There are many valuable resources in Denmark, but the more you know before you start, the easier the search becomes.

DANISH AMERICAN RESOURCES

Denmark is a constitutional monarchy of northwestern Europe consisting of a mainland and a large number of islands. The Danish language is part of the Scandinavian branch of the Teutonic family of Indo-European languages and shares many aspects in common with Norwegian, Swedish, and Icelandic.

Danish immigration in significant numbers began about the middle of the 19th century and continued late into the 1920s. There were early settlements in New York, particularly in Brooklyn and around the Finger Lakes region, and in New England in the areas of Portland, Maine and Boston.

However, the majority of settlers came to the Middle West with the first permanent colony in Waskauska County, Wisconsin occurring in 1845. Later, Racine, Wisconsin was to become a major center of Danish-American culture and remains so to this day. Eventually Danish pioneers settled throughout Wisconsin, Minnesota, Iowa, Nebraska, and the Dakotas. There was also a westward movement to Utah, Colorado, and Montana, and to the west coast cities of Los Angeles and Seattle.

While in most situations, Danes were an ethnic minorities, there were instances in which they were the dominant group as evidenced by towns like Dannebrog, Nebraska; Denmark, Wisconsin; St. Ansgar, Iowa; Danevang, Texas; and Solvang, California.

Danish immigrants established and maintain Dana College at Blair, Nebraska and Grand View College at Des Moines, Iowa, Along with Norwegians, they also founded Augsburg College in Minneapolis, and in cooperation with Norwegians and Swedes, the Trinity College and Evangelical Divinity School at Deerfield, Illinois.

DANISH IMMIGRANT MUSEUM
2212 Washington Street
Elk Horn, Iowa 51531
Tel. (712) 764-7001

This museum was established in 1983 and is dedicated to telling the story of the Danish-American experience from Westbrook, Maine to Greenville, Michigan to Dagmar, Montana to Ferndale, California. There are extensive family records with a staff who are prepared to help with searches for documents relating to the approximately 360,000 Danes who immigrated to America and Canada in the late 19th and early 20th centuries.

Elk Horn and neighboring Kimballton are predominantly Danish American communities and include such additional attractions as a windmill built in Denmark in 1848 and sent to Elk Horn in 1976, a restored bedstemor's (grandmother's) house used by early immigrants, plus numerous gift shops, bakeries, and restaurants featuring a Danish flavor. The Kimballton library also has a significant Danish-American historical collection.

DANISH IMMIGRANT ARCHIVES
Grand View College
Grand View Avenue
Des Moines, Iowa 50316
Tel. (515) 263-2877, Fax (515) 263-2998

Located in the library of Grand View College, their holdings include 57 feet of Danish and Danish-American newspapers and periodicals, 45 feet of immigrant literature and research publications, 24 feet of private individual collections, and 21 feet of files on individuals, families, communities, and fraternal organizations making it an outstanding resource for genealogical research.

He archives also has records of Danish-American folk school history, Lutheran Church publications, particularly those related to the Danish Evangelical Lutheran and the history of Grand View College which was founded by Danes in 1896.

They participate in DIAL (Danish Immigrant Archival Listing) which is an international reference system for locating records in the United States, Canada, and Denmark.

DANISH AMERICAN HERITAGE SOCIETY
4105 Stone Brooke Road
Ames, Iowa 50010
Tel. (541) 998-8562

This organization came into being in the 1970s to promote research in Danish-American history, particularly as it relates to the western United States. They publish a journal called *The Bridge* plus a semiannual newsletter. These publications contain manuscripts dealing with all aspects of the Danish immigrant experience in America.

They have recently moved to their present location in Iowa from Junction City, Oregon in order to facilitate a coordination of their historical interests with three other Danish-American historical organizations including the Danish immigrant Museum, Dana College library and Grand View College library. This plan will serve to promote more in-depth genealogical research as well as assist groups involved in the continuing work related to family histories and archival investigations.

Publications of the Danish American Heritage Society include:

The Bridge - twice a year historical journal
Favrhold, Visti. <u>Junction City to Denmark</u>
Hansen, Thorvald. <u>Danish Immigrant Archival Listing</u>
Mortensen, Enok. <u>A Danish Boyhood</u>
Mortensen, Enok. <u>Schools for Life: A Danish American Experiment in Adult Education</u>
Rasmussen, Gerald. <u>Oregon Danish Colony 1902-1952</u>

DANISH AMERICAN HISTORICAL ARCHIVES
Dana College
Blair, Nebraska 68008
Tel. (402) 426-7300, Fax (402) 426-7332

Located in the library of Dana College (founded in 1884 by the United Evangelical Lutheran Church) , their holdings include more than 1,000 books related to Denmark and Danish America. There is a collection of about 10,000 letters covering the period of 1870-1970 with information concerning Danish immigration, Dana College, various Danish folk high schools, plus photographs and records relating to early Danish settlers. A large hymnal collection is also part of the archives as are Bibles, psalmbooks, and other religious periodicals and literature relating to Danish-American communities and churches .

Publications of the Danish American Historical Archives:

Larsen, Birgit et al. <u>On Distant Shores</u>
Miller, Karen. <u>Many Danes, Some Norwegians</u>
Nielsen, John. <u>Tante Johanne: Letters of a Danish Immigrant Family</u>
Nielsen, Ruth. <u>Leaves and Acorns From Oaks</u>

DANISH BROTHERHOOD OF AMERICA
3717 Harney Street
Omaha, Nebraska 68131
Tel. (402) 341-5049, Fax (402) 341-0830

This is primarily a fraternal organization with 150 local branches scattered throughout the United States which are dedicated to the preservation of Danish-American heritage. They have an insurance program available to members as well as a college scholarship program. The Danish Brotherhood of America maintains some archival records which may be of value to the researcher.

They also publish a periodical called *The American Dane*.

ADDITIONAL DANISH LISTINGS:

DANISH AMERICAN FELLOWSHIP 4300 Cedar Ave., South Minneapolis, Minnesota 55407, Tel. (612) 729-3800

DANISH EMIGRATION ARCHIVES Email emiarch@vip.cybercity.dk http://www.cybercity.dk/users/ccc13656

SCANDINAVIAN GENEALOGICAL SOCIETY OF OREGON 1123 7th Street N.W. Salem, Oregon 97304

SEATTLE GENEALOGICAL SOCIETY 8511 15th Ave. N.E. Seattle, Washington 98111 Tel. (206) 522-8658

UNIVERSITY OF WASHINGTON LIBRARY MANUSCRIPTS ARCHIVES Box 352900 Seattle, Washington 98195, Tel. (206) 543-1879, Fax (206) 685-8723, Website --- http://www.lib.washington.edu

REGIONAL LIBRARIES WITH DANISH AMERICAN FAMILY RECORDS:

CEDAR FALLS HISTORICAL SOCIETY 303 Franklin, Cedar Falls, Iowa 50613, Tel. (319) 277-8817, Fax (319) 268-1812

ELK HORN PUBLIC LIBRARY 2027 Washington St., Elk Horn, Iowa 51531, Tel. (712) 764-2013

FRESNO COUNTY LIBRARY 2420 Mariposa St., Fresno, California 93721, Tel. (209) 488-3185 Fax (209) 488-1971 Website --- http//nc.sjuls.lib.ca.us.fresno

KIBALLTON PUBLIC LIBRARY Main St., Kimballton, Iowa 51543, Tel. (712) 773-3002

LUCK PUBLIC LIBRARY 21 Second St., Luck, Wisconsin 54853, Tel. (715) 472-2770

MAINE HISTORICAL SOCIETY 485 Congress, Portland, Maine 04101, Tel. (207) 774-1822, Fax (207) 775-4301

MINNEAPOLIS PUBLIC LIBRARY Tel. (612) 630-6000, Fax (612) 630-6210 Website --- http://www.mpls.lib.mn.us

STATE HISTORICAL SOCIETY OF IOWA 402 Iowa Ave, Iowa City, Iowa 52240, Tel. (319) 335-3916, Fax (319) 335-3935

UTAH STATE HISTORICAL SOCIETY 300 Rio Grande, Salt Lake City, Utah 84101, Tel. (801) 533-3535, Fax (801) 533- 3504

FINDING ANCESTORS IN FINLAND

Finland is divided into twelve provinces. Their names with their capitals in parentheses are:

1. Uudenmaan Lääni (Helsinki)
2. Turun Ja Porin Lääni (Turku)
3. Hameen Lääni (Hameenlinna)
4. Ahvenamaan Lääni (Mariehamn)
5. Kymen Lääni (Kouvola) *
6. Mikkelin Lääni (Mikkeli)
7. Kuopion Lääni (Kuopio)
8. Pohjois-Karjalan Lääni (Joensuu)
9. Keski-Suomen Lääni (Jyvaskyla)
10. Oulun Lääni (Oulu)
11. Lapin Lääni (Rovaniemi) *
12. Vaasan Lääni (Vaasa)

With the exception of the two marked by an asterisk, all of the provinces have their own archives.

The National Archives (Valtionaskisto) are located in the national capital city of Helsinki (PL 258, 00171 Helsinki).

The major religious groups maintain church records. The Lutheran Church registers go back to 1648, the Greek Orthodox to about 1779, and the Roman Catholic to 1800. There are over 500 parishes in Finland and more than 300 of them have now transferred their records to the National Archives and to various provincial archives.

Following is the major overall list of places to search for ancestors in Finland as outlined by Angus Baxter's book In Search of Your European Roots: A Complete Guide to Tracing Your Ancestors in Every Country in Europe.

1. Lutheran Church Registers. These records contain information on births, marriages, and deaths.

2. Greek Orthodox Church Registers also contain records of births, marriages, and deaths. Copies are also in the provincial archives at Mikkeli.

3. Catholic Church Registers have similar information as the Greek Orthodox Church Registers.

4. Lutheran Membership Movements are provincial records of persons arriving in a parish or leaving it.

5. Lutheran Pre-Confirmations. Some of these lists go back to 1696 and list children eligible for confirmation.

6. Tombstone Inscriptions. These have been recorded from the early 18th century by local churches and cemeteries.

7. Lutheran Main Books. These are probably the most comprehensive records to help ancestor hunting in Finland. They date back to 1667 and include many details about parishes and families

8. Civil Registration. Dating back to 1922, this is a list of those who are not members of the Lutheran Church.

9. Head Tax Registers. Records of a tax imposed in 1634 and abolished in 1924

10. Property Taxes. The provincial archives have copies of these lists from 1539 onward.

11. Guilds maintain records which are primarily in provincial archives

12. Wills and Probate Records. Some of these are in the National Archives and some in provincial archives. Wills are not too common in Finland due to the use of estate inventories.

13. Census Returns. Prior to 1925 only heads of families were named, but since that time, all members of the household are listed by name.

14. Land Records. These cover a period from 1630 to 1758 and are in the National Archives

15. Court Records. These not only include criminal cases, but also real estate and mortgage records. They are in the National Archives, provincial archives, and local court houses.

16. Register of the Inhabitants of Finland. This project lasted from 1539 until 1809 and contain much vital information now in the National Archives.

17. Military Records. These are rolls of military regiments from 1537 until 1909 and are in the War Archives in Helsinki and Stockholm.

18. Genealogical Society of Finland (Address is Suomen Sukutukimusseaura, Snellmaninkatu 9-11, 00170 Helsinki 17).

19. Lost Territories Archives include those areas lost to the Soviet Union and records of families who fled those territories. These records are in custody of the provincial archives of Mikkeil (Address is Lakkautetettujen Seurakuntien Keskusarkisto PL 78 50101 Mikkeli 10).

In terms of records going back at least 250 years, Finland is a genealogist's dream.

FINNISH AMERICAN RESOURCES

Finland is a republic of northern Europe bounded on the north by Norway and the Arctic Ocean, on the south by the Gulf of Finland, on the east by Russia, and on the west by Sweden and the Gulf of Bothnia.

Finnish is a subdivision of the Finno-Ugric branch of the Ural Altaic languages and has much in common with both Estonian and Hungarian.

While Finnish immigrants first came to the United States with the Swedish settlers on the Delaware in the 1630s large scale immigration did not begin until the 1860s. While a few settled in Boston, New York, and Philadelphia, the majority came to the upper peninsula of Michigan, the to the northern counties of Wisconsin and Minnesota, and to the sections of the Pacific Northwest, particularly around Portland, Oregon and Seattle, Washington.

The towns of Marquette, Ishpeming, Negaunee, Hancock, and Ironwood in the upper peninsula of Michigan have very large Finnish populations as do Ely, Hibbing, Sebeka, and Duluth in northeastern Minnesota. The area surrounding Astoria, Oregon and the Olympic Peninsula in Washington attracted considerable numbers of Finnish settlers as did the northern California towns of Eureka and Reedley, and the Rocky Mountain areas of Red Lodge, Montana and Rock Springs, Wyoming.

Finnish immigration to the east was concentrated in Massachusetts, particularly around Fitchburg and Gardner, with some also in Maine near South Paris. The Lake Erie communities of Ashtabula, Conneaut, and Fairport Harbor, Ohio also have large Finnish population.

Finlandia University in Hancock, Michigan (originally Suomi College) was founded in 1896 by Finnish immigrants of the former Finnish Evangelical Lutheran Church (Suomi Synod) which is now part of the Evangelical Lutheran Church in America.

FINLANDIA UNIVERSITY LIBRARY
Quincy Street
Hancock, Michigan 49930
Tel. (906) 482-5300
Fax (906) 487-7366
Website --- http://www.suomi.edu/ink/

The university was founded in 1896 by Finnish settlers and serves as the national hub for Finnish American culture. It is the only institution of higher learning in the United States established by Finns.

The library has many volumes in both Finnish and English related to Finnish life and culture in America and Canada including records of Finnish churches, family records, and Finnish church and civil news periodicals that have been published in both languages over the last century. A significant collection of books on Finnish language and literature is maintained here as well and the university has a major program in Finnish Studies.

The university library coordinates its historical work and resources with the Finnish American Heritage Society located in a building adjacent to the campus.

FINNISH AMERICAN HERITAGE CENTER
601 Quincy Street
Hancock, Michigan 49930
Tel. (906) 487-7347
Fax (906) 476-7366

Located adjacent to the campus of Finlandia University, the center dates back to 1932. Many of its records were located in the university library until 1990 when it purchased and renovated a former Catholic Church.

The archives contain more than 7,000 books plus 660 tapes, 186 periodicals, and 107 newspaper titles as well as family records, personal papers, and photographs. There are also extensive records relating to the Suomi Synod, the Finnish National Brotherhood of Temperance Societies and records of Suomi College. The museum has historical artifacts of early industry in the area and a theatre provides cultural and educational opportunities.

SWEDISH FINN HISTORICAL SOCIETY
6512 23rd Ave. N.W.
Seattle, Washington 98117-5728
Tel. (206) 789-3271

This society was founded in 1991 by a small group of descendants of Swedish-speaking Finns desiring to preserve their cultural heritage.

Their holdings include more than 500 books in an archives and genealogy center which has oral histories and family genealogiesas well as includes newspapers, newsletters, periodicals, and other documents of historical and cultural value particularly relating to Swedish Finns of the Pacific Northwest.The society is also the repository for the International Order of Runeberg.

FINNISH AMERICAN HISTORICAL SOCIETY OF THE WEST
P.O. Box 5522
Portland, Oregon 97208
Tel. (503) 654-0448
Website --- http://www.teleport.com/finnamhs

Archival materials and family records of this group on focus on Finnish settlements in the American west, particularly Washington, Oregon, and northern California. The group promotes historical research, collects pioneers stories and artifacts, commemorates noteworthy sites, and works for the preservation of the Finnish language and ethnic traditions.

Organized in 1962 the FAHSW is engaged in an active publishing program of books relating to Finnish Americana including histories of settlements in the west. Their publications include:

The Lewis River Finns
The Pendleton River Finns
The Pioneer Finnish Home
The Theatre Finns
Finnish Lutherans in the Melting Pot
Finns of Winlock
Coal-Mining Finns of Washington State
Blue Mountain Finns
Centerville Finns
Finns of Hoquiam and Aberdeen

ADDITIONAL FINNISH LISTINGS:

FAMILY SLEUTHS P.O. Box 525163, Salt Lake City, Utah 84152, Tel. (801) 467-4201

FINLAND HISTORICAL SOCIETY County Road #135, Finland, Minnesota 55603, Tel. (208) 353-7393

FINN CREEK MUSEUM P.O. Box 134, New York Mills, Minnesota 56567, Tel. (208) 385-2200

FINNISH AMERICAN HERITAGE SOCIETY OF MAINE Box 249, West Paris, Maine 04289, Tel. (207) 674-3094

FINNISH GENEALOGY GROUP 2119 21st Avenue, Minneapolis, Minnesota 55404, Tel. (602) 333-6028

FITCHBURG STATE COLLEGE LIBRARY Highland Ave., Fitchburg, Massachusetts 01420, Tel. (508) 665-3194, Fax (508) 665-3069 Website --- http://www.fsc.edu/library/

MINNESOTA FINNISH AMERICAN HISTORICAL SOCIETY Rt 3 Box 312, Sebeka, Minnesota 56477

SAMPO PUBLICATIONS P.O. Box 102804, New Brighton, Minnesota 55112, Tel. (602) 636-6348

SCANDINAVIAN GENEALOGICAL SOCIETY OF OREGON 1123 7th Street N.W., Salem, Oregon 97304

SEATTLE GENEALOGICAL SOCIETY 8511 15th Avenue N.E., Seattle, Washington 98111, Tel. (206) 522-8658

UNIVERSITY OF WASHINGTON LIBRARY Manuscripts and University Archives, Box 352900, Seattle, Washington 98195, Tel. (206) 543-1760, Fax (206) 685-8727, Website --- http://www.lib.washington.edu

REGIONAL LIBRARIES WITH FINNISH AMERICAN FAMILY RECORDS:

ASHTABULA COUNTY LIBRARY 335 W. 44th St., Ashtabula, Ohio 44004, Tel. (440) 997-9341, Fax (440) 992-7714

ASTORIA PUBLIC LIBRARY 450 10th St. Astoria, Oregon 97103, Tel. (503) 325-7323, Fax (503) 325-2017

DULUTH PUBLIC LIBRARY 520 W. Superior St., Duluth, Minnesota 55802, Tel. (208) 723 3821, Fax (208) 723-3815

FAIRPORT PUBLIC LIBRARY 335 Vine St., Fairport Harbor, Ohio 44077, Tel. (206) 354-8191, Fax (206) 354-6059

HUMBOLDT COUNTY LIBRARY 636 F Street, Eureka, California 95501, Tel. (707) 269-1900, Fax (707) 269-1997

NEW YORK PUBLIC LIBRARY 5th Ave & 42nd St., New York, New York 10018, Tel. (212) 930-0810, Fax (212) 921-2546

NORTHERN MICHIGAN UNIVERSITY LIBRARY 1401 Presque Isle, Marquette, Michigan 49855, Tel. (906) 227-2117, Fax (906) 227-1333

PETER WHITE PUBLIC LIBRARY 217 N. Front St., Marquette, Michigan 49855, Tel. (906) 228-9510, Fax (906) 228-7315

PHOEBE APPERSON HEARST LIBRARY Lead, South Dakota 57754, Tel. (605) 584-2013

TIMBERLAND REGIONAL LIBRARY 415 Airindustrail, Olympia, Washington 98501, Tel. (360) 943-5001, Fax (360) 586-6838

FINDING ANCESTORS IN ICELAND

Iceland is divided into various municipal units. There are 200 counties (hreppur) and several of these are grouped into a region (sysla) of which there are 19. The 16 major towns are excluded from this system. Sources of genealogical information listed in Baxter's aforementioned resources include the following:

1. Civil Registration. This started in 1735 when Lutheran pastors recorded the vital events of each parish and supplied the bishop with a copy. The system was replaced by the National Register in 1953.

2. Censuses. The first took place in 1703 and there have been additional ones in 1729, 1801, 1835, 1840, 1845, 1855, 1860, and every ten years to 1901. Records are in the National Archives.

3. The National Register. This was started in 1953 and includes immigration and emigration records. Which are kept by the Statistical Bureau of Iceland (Hagstofa Islands) Hverfisgata 101 Reykjavik.

4. Church Registers. Many, but not all, of these are in the National Archives and many recent ones are also in parish churches.

5. Confirmations. These date from 1830 to the present, Records up to 1958 are in the National Archives and more recent ones are with parish churches. The address of the Evangelical Lutheran Church of Iceland (to which 94 percent of the population belong) is Biskup Islands Klapparstig 27, 101 Reykjavik.

6. Church Censuses. These have been held at irregular intervals from 1790 to the present and include persons arriving at and leaving parishes/

7. Ministerial Biographies. These include biographical information on clergy dating back to the 11th century.

8. Wills. The National Archives contain wills from 1717 to 1937. Later years are in the custody of the local courts.

9. Mortgages. These date from 1700s and up to 1900 are in the National Archives, Since that time they are in the local courts.

10. Court records. These started in 1619 and include criminal and civil cases as well as property settlements and are in the National Archives.

Watch out for patronymics. Iceland is the most difficult of all Scandinavian nations to trace names since every citizen is entitled to two names. In a telephone directory people may be listed under the first letter of their Christian name.

ICELANDIC AMERICAN RESOURCES

Iceland is an island in the north Atlantic having about 200,000 inhabitants. Most speak the Icelandic language which is a Scandinavian language that is related to Norwegian, Danish, and Swedish.

Migration from Iceland to the united States has not occurred in very large numbers and there are probably less than 20,000 Icelanders living in the United States and Canada. While the city of Winnipeg, Manitoba in Canada has been the North American center for Icelandic colonization, there are also several U.S. Cities with Icelandic communities including Chicago, Minneapolis, Seattle, and Tacoma.

In addition to Minneapolis, the small town of Minneota, Minnesota is home to a group of Icelanders as are several small towns in North Dakota and the town of Blaine in the state of Washington.

But the largest Icelandic community in the United States is in Seattle where the Ballard section of that city serves as a hub for Icelandic cultural activities designed to preserve the traditions of the homeland.

Hallgrim's Icelandic Church, Seattle. This photograph is one of many in Dr. Larson's collection at Everett Psychiatric Clinic.

EVERETT PSYCHIATRIC CLINIC
3731 Colby St.
Everett, Washington 98201
Tel. (206) 252-3557

Under the direction of Dr. William Larson of the clinic, the collection on Iceland and Icelandic America has grown to more than 12,000 books and manuscripts. Materials on Nordic mythology and Scandinavian immigrant history are available.

Archival material consists of personal family letters from Iceland to turn-of-the-century immigrants in the Pacific Northwest and western Canada. There is also a substantial collection of photographs depicting Icelandic-American activities of the early days plus genealogical documents relating to Danes and Norwegians in the area as well.

ADDITIONAL ICELANDIC LISTINGS:

SEATTLE GENEALOGICAL SOCIETY 8511 15th Ave. N.E., Seattle, Washington 98111, Tel. (206) 522-8658

SCANDINAVIAN GENEALOGICAL SOCIETY OF OREGON 1123 7th St. N.W., Salem, Oregon 97304

UNIVERSITY OF NORTH DAKOTA - CHESTER FRITZ LIBRARY Box 9000, Grand Forks, North Dakota 58202-9000, Tel. (701) 777-4625, Website --- http://www.und.nodak.edu/dept/library

UNIVERSITY OF WASHINGTON LIBRARY Manuscripts and University Archives, Box 352900, Seattle, Washington 98195, Tel. (206) 543-1760, Fax (206) 685-8727, Website --- http://www.libr.washington.edu

REGIONAL LIBRARIES WITH ICELANDIC AMERICAN FAMILY RECORDS:

CHICAGO PUBLIC LIBRARY 400 S. State St., Chicago. Illinois 60605, Tel. (312) 747-4999, Fax (312) 747-4962, Website --- http://cpl/lib.uic.edu

MINNESOTA HISTORICAL SOCIETY 690 Cedar St., St. Paul, Minnesota 55101, Website --- http://www.mnhs.org

TACOMA PUBLIC LIBRARY 1102 Tacoma Ave., Tacoma, Washington 98402 ,Tel. (206) 591-5666, Fax (206) 591-5470

NORTH DAKOTA STATE UNIVERSITY LIBRARY 1301 12th Ave., Fargo, North Dakota 58105, Tel. (701) 231-8886, Fax (701) 231-7138, Website --- http://www.lib.ndsu.nodak.edu

FINDING ANCESTORS IN NORWAY

There are two forms of Norwegian language - Bokmål, used in book language, and Nynorsk, the so-called country language. The nation is divided into 18 counties plus the capital district of Oslo. Some have changed their names so the following list includes the old names on parentheses as they may be necessary for ancestor hunting:

1. Akerhus
2. Aust-Agder (Nedenes)
3. Buskerud
4. Finnmark
5. Hedemark
6. Hordaland (Søndre Bergenhus)
7. Møre og Romsdal (Søndre Trondheim)
8. Nordland
9. Nord-Trøndelag (Nordre Trondheim)
10. Oppland (Christian)
11. Oslo (Christiania)
12. Østfold (Smaalene)
13. Rogaland (Ryfylke)
14. Sogn og Fjordane (Nodre Bergenhus)
15. Telemark (Bratsberg)
16. Troms (Tromsø)
17. Vest Agder (lister og Mandal)
18. Vestfold (Jarlsberg or Larvik)

The National Archives of Norway are called the Riksarkivet and are located at Folke Bernadottes vei 21, Postboks 20, Kingjå, Oslo. In addition, there are six regional archives located at:
1. Oslo to cover Ostfold, Akerhus, Buskerud, Vestfold, and Telemark
2. Hamar to cover Hedmark and Oppland
3. Kristiansund to cover Aust-Agder and Vest-Agder
4. Stavanger to cover Rogaland
5. Bergen to cover Hordaland and Sognor Fjordane

6. Trondheim to cover Møre og Romsdal, Sør Trøndelag, Nord Trøndelag Nordland, Troms, and Finnmark

Angus Baxter's book lists the following genealogical sources in Norway:

1. Parish Records. Many localities in Norway have village books which have valuable information about families in the parish.

2. Church Records. Registration of births, marriages, an deaths is primarily the responsibility of the Lutheran Church. These records are transferred to the regional archives after 8 years.

3. Census Returns. These date back to 1664 and may be the best in Europe. They are in both the National Archives and in regional archives.

4. Probate Registers. These are primarily real estate transfers dating back to 1660.

5. Registers of Conveyances and Mortgages. These are real estate transactions mainly in local archives or local town clerks.

6. Real Estate Books. These date from 1665 and are mainly in the National Archives.

7. Court Records have some criminal, but mainly civil, records and are in the National Archives.

8. Tax Lists. These go back to 1645 and are in both regional archives and the National Archives.

9. Lists of Emigrants include police lists and ship lists. They are in police stations as well as various regional archives.

10. Military Records date from 1634 to the present and are in regional archives as well as town halls.

11. Guild Records. If your ancestor was a craftsman, you may look him up in trade guild records generally in local city archives.

One additional help in tracing Norwegian ancestors is the Data Arkivet, Universitet Tromsø, 9001 Tromsø. Knowing places of origin is important since there are so many overlapping common Norwegian names.

NORWEGIAN AMERICAN RESOURCES

Norway, along with Sweden and Finland, form the Scandinavian peninsula. It is inhabited by four million people who speak two dialects of Norwegian, a language belonging to the Scandinavian subfamily of Indo-Germanic languages and closely related to Danish, Swedish, and Icelandic.

Norwegian immigration in significant numbers began in the 1830s and continued into the 1920s. Early settlers came to New York, but the majority went to Wisconsin, Minnesota, Iowa, and the Dakotas. Later migration also went to the Rocky Mountain states and to the west coast.

There has been a tendency among Norwegian immigrants to avoid large cities with the exceptions of Brooklyn, Chicago, Minneapolis, and Seattle.

The cities of Madison, Milwaukee, Eau Clair, and Superior, Wisconsin have large Norwegian populations while Minneapolis, St. Paul, Austin, and Duluth, Minnesota are cities in that state with significant numbers of Norwegians as are Fargo and Jamestown, North Dakota, and Sioux Falls in South Dakota.

Norwegians have established numerous colleges including St. Olaf at Northfield, Concordia at Moorhead, Bethany at Mankato, and Augsburg at Minneapolis, all in Minnesota. They also founded Luther College at Decorah and Waldorf at Forest City, both in Iowa and Augustana College ar Sioux Falls, South Dakota.

In addition, Pacific Lutheran University at Tacoma, Washington and the Luther-Northwestern Theological Seminary at St. Paul, Minnesota were established by Norwegians. Along with the Danes and the Swedes they also helped to found the Trinity College and Evangelical Divinity School at Deerfield, Illinois.

Photo courtesy of Augsburg College

AUGSBURG COLLEGE
George Sverdrup Library
2211 Riverdale Ave.
Minneapolis, Minnesota 55454
Tel. (612) 330-1604
Fax (612) 330-1446
Website --- http://www.augsburg.edu/library

The college was founded in 1869 by Norwegians and Danes of the Lutheran faith who became part of the Lutheran Free Church.

There are many historical records in the George Sverdrup Library of early Scandinavian settlements and family and parishes, particularly relating to the Upper Midwest, i.e. Wisconsin, Minnesota, and the Dakotas.

The library also has collections of Bibles, hymnals in Norwegian, Danish, and English.

NORWEGIAN AMERICAN HISTORICAL ASSOCIATION
Rolvaag Memorial Library
St. Olaf College
Northfield, Minnesota 55057
Tel. (507) 646-3221 Fax, (507) 646-3734
Website --- http://www.stolaf.edu/stolaf/othel/naha.htm

St. Olaf was founded by Norwegian Lutherans in 1874 and has served as a hub for Norwegian American culture in the upper midwest. Located in the college library, the association has,for 75 years , served as a repository for documents related to immigration and settlement of Norwegians in America

The NAHA has more than 8,000 books in its holdings plus cores of diaries, journals, family, and church histories along with photographs that document Norwegian American life.   It also engages in a vigorous publishing program which include book that chronicle many facets of Norwegian life in the United States. Archival collections date back to 1865.

Publications of the NAHA include:

Bjork, Kenneth. Saga and Steel in Concrete
Blegen, T. Frontier Mother: the Letters of Gro Svendsen
Clausen, C. A Chronicler of Immigrant Life
Hamre, James. George Sverdrup: Educator,Theologian, Churchman
Hustvedt, Lloyd. Guide to Manuscripts of the Naha
Larson,Lawrence. The Log Book of a Young Immigrant
Lokke, Carl. Klondike Saga
Lovoll, Odd. A History of the Norwegian American People
Wefald, Jon A Voice of Protest: Norwegians in American Politics

LUTHER COLLEGE
Preus Library
Decorah, Iowa 52101
Tel. (319) 387-2000, Fax (319) 387-2158
Website --- http://www.luther.edu

The college was founded by Norwegian Lutherans and its Preus Library has significant holdings of Norwegian Americana in the Midwest.

VESTERHEIM GENEALOGICAL SOCIETY
502 Water Street
Decorah, Iowa 52101
Tel.(319) 382-9681, Fax (319) 382-8828

This center has valuable family records and genealogy materials dating back to the 1870s including passport records on microfiche and hundreds of microfilms of Norwegian church records It also has an excellent collection of Norwegian community histories, as well as emigrant lists, passenger lists, and membership rolls of Norwegian background churches.

There are more than 1,700 books on Norwegian America plus 1,200 microfilms. The center serves as a clearinghouse for genealogical inquiries and offers guidance to researchers.

SONS OF NORWAY INTERNATIONAL LIBRARY
1455 W. Lake Street
Minneapolis, Minnesota 55408
Tel. (602) 827-3611, Fax (602) 827-0068

This fraternal and cultural organization was founded in 1962 to foster fellowship, provide insurance, and sponsor recreational activities through its 400 locally-governed lodges. It maintains a library of 2,500 volumes dealing with Norwegian American life and also has immigration records that are a valuable resource for the genealogical researcher.

A periodical newsletter called the *Viking* is sent to all members.

CONCORDIA COLLEGE
Carl B. Ylvisaker Library
Moorhead, Minnesota 56562
Tel. (218) 299-4640, Fax (218) 299-4253
Website --- http://www.cord.edu.dep/library/

The college was founded in 1891 by Norwegian immigrants who settled in northern Minnesota and North Dakota. Their holdings include a significant collection of records relating to families who came to the area and to the churches established in the area near the turn of the century Archival records include oral histories, personal correspondence, congregational histories, and other monographs relating to Norwegian American culture in the area plus documents relating to the history of Concordia College.

AUGUSTANA COLLEGE
Mikkelsen Library
Sioux Falls, South Dakota 57197
Tel. (605) 336-4921, Fax (605) 336-5447
Website --- http://inst.augie.edu/

This college was founded in 1860 by Norwegian immigrants who came to South and North Dakota. The Mikkelsen Library has A sizable Norwegian collection of documents relating to these pioneers including family and church records, plus Bibles, hymnals, and other data in both Norwegian and English. The archives are open to the public for purposes of genealogical research.

LUTHERAN BRETHREN SCHOOLS LIBRARY
Vernon Ave.
Fergus Falls, Minnesota 56537
Tel. (218) 739 -3375, Fax (218) 739-3372

This educational institution was founded by the Church of the Lutheran Brethren, a small Norwegian-background group in the early 1900s. It has preserved records of Norwegian families and churches of that particular synod primarily in Wisconsin, Minnesota, and the Dakotas.

BETHANY LUTHERAN COLLEGE LIBRARY
734 Marsh Street
Mankato, Minnesota 56001-4490
Tel. (507) 386-5349, Fax (507) 386-5376
 Website http://www.edu/blc/lib/mainframe.html

The college was founded in 1927 by the Norwegian Synod of the Lutheran Church. It maintains family and church records of Norwegian communities and churches primarily in the upper midwest as well as historical records of the college and the theological seminary which occupies the same campus.

The library participates in Online Pub Access Catalog (OPAC) and in the Minnesota Interlibrary Telecommunication Exchange.

PACIFIC LUTHERAN UNIVERSITY
Robert A. L. Mortvedt Library
S. 121st St. and Park Ave. S.
Tacoma, Washington 98447
Tel (253) 535-7500, Fax (253) 535-7315
Website --- http://www.plu.edu/libr/library.html/

The university was founded in 1894 and has acted as a center for Scandinavian culture in the Pacific Northwest. The Scandinavian Immigrant Collection is an outstanding source for research into the early history of Nordic immigrants to the area.

Family records, personal letters, and church histories are all part of the collection as are oral histories.

LUTHER-NORTHWESTERN THEOLOGICAL SEMINARY LIBRARY
2375 Como Avenue
St. Paul, Minnesota 55108
Tel (602) 641-3224, Fax (602) 641-3280
Website --- http://www.luthersem.edu/library

This school was established in 1876 to train clergy for the Norwegian Evangelical Lutheran Church, now part of the larger Evangelical Lutheran Church in America. It maintains records of Norwegian immigration and Norwegian congregations primarily in the Upper Midwest.

ADDITIONAL NORWEGIAN LISTINGS:

COON VALLEY RESEARCH AT NORSKEDALEN P.O. Box 225, Coon Valley, Wisconsin 54623, Tel. (608) 452-3424

LITTLE NORWAY INC. 3576 Highway JG-N, Blue Mounds, Wisconsin 53517, Tel. (608) 437-8211

NORWEGIAN GENEALOGICAL GROUP 106 19th Ave S.E., Minneapolis, Minnesota 55414

SCANDINAVIAN GENEALOGICAL SOCIETY OF OREGON 1123 7th Street N.W., Salem, Oregon 97304

SEATTLE GENEALOGICAL SOCIETY 8511 15th Ave N.E., Seattle, Washington 98111, Tel. (206) 522-8658

UNIVERSITY OF NORTH DAKOTA Chester Fritz Library, Box 9000, Grand Forks, North Dakota 58202-9000, Tel. (701) 777-2617, Fax (701) 777-3319, Website --- http://www.und.nodak.edu/dept/library

UNIVERSITY OF WASHINGTON LIBRARY Manuscripts and University Archives, Box 352900, Seattle, Washington 98195, Tel. (206) 543-1760, Fax (206) 685-8727, Website --- http://www,lib.washington.edu

VALDRES SAMBAND LAG 1522 North Greenwood Court, North Eagan, Minnesota 55122, Email: bettylou@ spacestar.net

REGIONAL LIBRARIES WITH NORWEGIAN AMERICAN FAMILY RECORDS:

CHICAGO PUBLIC LIBRARY 400 S. State St. ,Chicago, Illinois 60605, Tel. (302) 747-4999, Fax (311) 747-4962, Website --- http://cpl/lib.uic.edu

DECORAH PUBLIC LIBRARY 202 Winnebago, Decorah, Iowa 52101, Tel. (319) 382-3717, Fax (319) 382-6524

MINNEAPOLIS PUBLIC LIBRARY 300 Nicollet Mall, Minneapolis, Minnesota 55401, Tel. (602) 630-6000, Fax (602) 630-6210

MINNESOTA HISTORICAL SOCIETY 690 Cedar St., St. Paul, Minnesota 55101, Website --- http://www.mnhs.org

MUSKEGO PUBLIC LIBRARY Racine Ave., Muskego, Wisconsin 53150 TEL (414) 679-4120 FAX (414) 679-4123

NEW YORK PUBLIC LIBRARY 5th Ave & 42nd Street, New York, New York 10018, Tel. (212) 930-0800, Fax (212) 921-2546, Website --- http://www.nypl.org

NORTH DAKOTA STATE UNIVERSITY LIBRARY 1301 12th Ave, Fargo, North Dakota 58105, Website --- http://www.lib.ndsu.nodak.edu

PETERSBURG PUBLIC LIBRARY Box 549, Petersburg, Alaska 99833, Tel. (907) 772-3344, Fax (907) 772-3759

SOUTH DAKOTA STATE HISTORICAL SOCIETY 900 Governors Ave., Pierre, South Dakota 57501, Tel. (605) 773-3804, Fax (605) 773-6041, Website --- http://www.state.sd.us/state/culturalarchives.html

FINDING ANCESTORS IN SWEDEN

Ancestor hunting in Sweden is probably the easiest in Europe. But you will need to know the name of the parish from which they came since there are more than 2,000 parishes in Sweden. The country is divided into 24 counties (län). In seven counties there are archives known as Landsarkivet.

The counties in Sweden include (with abbreviations):

1. Älvsborg (Elfsborg) P
2. Blekinge K
3. Gotland I
4. Gävleborg X
5. Göteborg and Bohus O
6. Halland N
7. Jämtland Z
8. Jönköping F
9. Kalmar H
10. Kopparberg W
11. Kristiansted L
12. Kronoborg G
13. Malmöhus M
14. Norrbotten BD
15. Örebro T
16. Östergötland E
17. Skaraborg R
18. Södermanland D
19. Stockholm B
20. Uppsala C
21. Värmland S
22. Västerbotten AC
23. Västernorrland Y
24. Västmanland U

Like the other Scandinavian entries, the author is indebted to the listing in Angus Baxter's reference. Following are the Swedish resources:

1. Church Registers. Some church records go back as far as 1607. Most have been transferred from individual churches to the regional archives.

2. Personal Records. This information on the population is maintained by the Central Bureau of Statistics.

3. Censuses. These started in 1620. Copies are in the Cameral Archives in Stockholm.

4. Property Lists date back to 1540 and record all transactions in property. They are kept in the regional archives.

5. Probate Records. These are inventories of real property as well as personal property of deceased persons. They are in regional archives and in district courts.

6. Tax Lists only existed from 1640-42 and are located in the Cameral Archives in Stockholm.

7, Court Records. These comprehensive records go back to 1620 and have details of court cases and prosecutions as well as real estate information.

8. Trade Guilds. These cover the period from 1640 to 1890 and are usually found in city archives.

9. Emigration Records. Nearly all emigrants from Sweden passed through the ports of Malmö and Göteborg. To do so they had to register with the police. These records are in both regional and city archives as well as with the Central Bureau of Statistics in Stockholm.

Finally, your search for Swedish ancestors may be helped by two active genealogical organizations. They are:

Personhistorika Samfundet
Riksarkivet 100 26 Stockholm

and

Genealogiska Föreningen
Arkivgaten 3, 111 28 Stockholm

From all these sources you should be able to find out much about your emigrant ancestor. But, as in any search, the more you know prior to starting the search, the easier the trip becomes.

SWEDISH AMERICAN RESOURCES

Sweden is the largest of the Scandinavian countries in both area and population. It is bound on the west by Norway and on the east by Finland. The Swedish language belongs to the eastern group of Scandinavian languages and is related to Norwegian, Danish, and Icelandic.

While Swedish colonists arrived on the Delaware in 1638, a consistent tide of immigration did not occur until the 1840s and continued through the early part of the 20th century. Original migration was to such eastern cities as Boston, Providence, and Hartford. The movement also spread to western New York around Jamestown and to western Pennsylvania. Other settlements were along Lake Erie in Ashtabula and Cleveland,but the largest Swedish migration came to Illinois, Minnesota, Iowa, Wisconsin, and Nebraska.

Chicago and Minneapolis became major centers of Swedish-American culture. Rockford, Illinois vied with Jamestown, New York as being the most Swedish city in the United States. Omaha, Nebraska and Denver, Colorado received large numbers of Swedes as did the Pacific Northwest cities of Portland, Oregon and Seattle, Washington.

Some rural communities in America have names which indicate their Swedish heritage such as Stockholm, Maine; Gothenburg, Nebraska; Swea City, Iowa; and Lindsborg, Kansas.

Swedish Pioneers established such educational institutions as Gustavus Adolphus College in St. Peter and Bethel College in St. Paul, Minnesota; North Park college and Seminary in Chicago and Augustana College in Rock Island, Illinois; Bethany College in Lindsborg, Kansas; and along with Danes and Norwegians, the Trinity College and Evangelical Divinity School in Deerfield, Illinois.

38

THE AMERICAN SWEDISH
INSTITUTE
2600 Park Ave
Minneapolis,Minnesota 55407
Tel. (612) 871-4907
Fax (612) 871-8686

The institute is located in the Swan Turnblad Mansion, a turn-of-the century interpretation of stately Romanesque chateau architecture composed of 33 rooms.

It serves as a center for Swedish-American cultural affairs in the upper Midwest. Within its elegantly appointed rooms are displayed social and cultural artifacts spanning over 150 years of the Swedish experience in America.

The holdings also include a library with family records of early Swedes in Minnesota as well as a book store. Special schools offering instruction in the Swedish language are given on a regular basis with goal of preserving ethnic culture.

AMERICAN SWEDISH HISTORICAL FOUNDATION
1900 Pattison Avenue
Philadelphia, Pennsylvania 19145
Tel. (215) 289-1776, Fax (215) 289-7701
Website --- http://www.libertynet.org/ashm

The Foundation is housed in a building modelled after the 17th century Eriksberg Castle in Sodermanland,Sweden. There are more than 11,000 volumes in its library mostly related to the emigration of Swedes to the colonies including establishment of the two "Old Swedes" churches still active in Wilmington,Delaware and in Philadelphia.

There is a significant collection of genealogical material to assist those engaged in research. Archives concentration the period from 1492 to 1865.

THE SWEDISH AMERICAN HISTORICAL SOCIETY
5125 North Spaulding
Chicago, Illinois 60625
Tel. (773) 583-5722, Fax (773) 267-2362
Website --- http://www.northpark.edu/library/swedish-americanhistory

The Society began in 1948 emerging out of the Swedish Pioneer Centennial Association. Its purpose is to stimulate and promote interest in Swedish-American contributions to the history and growth of the United States.

There is a collection of more than 3,000 books plus 6,000 unbound documents, and 3,500 microfiche. There are also documents relating to the early history of the Swedish Mission (now Evangelical Covenant) Church.
Publications include:

Hasselmo, Nils. Perspectives of Swedish Immigration
Homes, Alvin. Swedish Homesteaders in Idaho
Johansson, Carl-Erik. Cradled in Sweden
Ljungmark, Lars. Swedish Exodus
Olsson, Nils. Tracing Your Swedish Ancestry
Westerberg, O. Guide to Swedish-American Archival and Manuscript
    Sources in the United States

SWEDISH COLONIAL SOCIETY
1300 Locust Street
Philadelphia, Pennsylvania 19107
Tel. (215) 688-0425

This is the oldest Scandinavian historical society in America. It was organized in 1908, but has records dating back to the 1640s. The society is also involved in the restoration and preservation of historic landmarks relating to Swedish accomplishments in America.

Several books have been published which include:

Johnson, Amandus. The Swedish Contribution to American Freedom
Johnson, Amandus. The Swedish Settlements on the Delaware
Tornquist, Karl G. The Naval Campaign of Count de Grasse

GUSTAVUS ADOLPHUS COLLEGE
Folke Bernadotte Library
St. Peter, Minnesota 56082
Tel. (507) 933-7552, Fax (507) 933-6292
Website --- http://www.gac.edu/library

Founded in 1862 by Swedish Lutherans and named after a Swedish king, the college maintains a significant collection of materials relating to Swedish settlements in the upper Midwest and is under the direction of a full-time archivist.

Archives date back to the 1850s and also contain documents relating to the history of the college.

BAPTIST GENERAL CONFERENCE ARCHIVES
3949 Bethel Dr.
St. Paul, Minnesota 55112
Tel. (612) 638-6222, Fax (612) 638-6001
Website --- http://www.bethel.edu

This center has many valuable documents relating to the history of early Swedish Baptists in America and is located on the campus of Bethel

College. There are more than 1,000 books in its collection with archival records of families, leaders, and churches written in both Swedish and English.

The Skarstedt Collection in Pietism also contains documents relating to early Swedish Baptist work in America

AUGUSTANA HISTORICAL SOCIETY
Augustana College Library
Rock Island, Illinois 61201
Tel. (309) 794-7266, Fax (309) 794-7230
Website --- http://www.augustana,edu/library

Since its founding in 1930 this Society has traced the stories of Swedish pioneers in the Midwestern states. They have published a number of books and also maintain the national records of the former Augustana Evangelical Lutheran Church which is now part of the larger Evangelical Lutheran Church in America. Here are also parish records and histories of the early Swedish clergy.

Their publications include:

Ander, O.F. Vision for a Valley
Ander, O.F. The American Origin of the Augustana Synod
Bergendoff, Conrad. The Augustana Ministerium
Bergendoff, Conrad. The Church of Sweden on the Delaware
Bergendoff, Conrad. The Pioneer Swedish Settlements
Eklund, E. Peter Fjellstad: Missionary Mentor to Three Continents
Lindquist, Emor. Smoky Valley People
Naeseth, H.C.K. The Swedish Theatre of Chicago
Swan, G.N. Swedish American Literary Periodicals

NORTH PARK UNIVERSITY LIBRARY
3225 West Foster Ave.
Chicago, Illinois 60625
Tel. (773) 244-5500 or (800) 888-6728

The college and seminary were established in 1891 by the Swedish

Mission (now Evangelical Covenant) Church. The library maintains a sizable collection of Scandinavian materials including family and congregational records from early Swedish Mission Churches.

This is a good source of material for Swedish family records and immigration history in the greater Chicago area.

SWENSON SWEDISH IMMIGRATION RESEARCH CENTER
639 38th St.
Rock Island, Illinois 60201
Tel. (309) 794-7204, Fax (309) 794-7443
Website --- http://www.viking.augustana.edu/admin/swenson

The Center has more than 9,000 books on Swedish America, plus 1,000 bound periodicals and more than 1,500 reels of historical data. There are also documents related to the Swedish lutheran, the Swedish mission covenant, the Evangelical free, the Swedish Methodist, and Swedish General Conference Baptist Churches.

In addition to a large collection of genealogical material, they also have passenger lists from the ports of Goteborg, Malmo, Kalmar, Stockholm, and Norkoping in Sweden plus Kristiania, Oslo, and Bergen in Norway.

The center has an active genealogical research program and will assist those who request it.

BETHANY COLLEGE
Wallerstedt Library
235 E. Swensson St.
Lindsborg, Kansas 67456
Tel. (917) 227-331

This college was founded by Swedish immigrants who settled in Kansas and has roots dating back to 1907.

Its historical collection includes family and church records dating back to the turn of the century in both Swedish and English. It works with the Lindsborg Community Library which also has a significant Scandinavian collection.

ADDITIONAL SWEDISH LISTINGS:

AMERICAN FRIENDS OF SWEDISH EMIGRANT INSTITUTE 3452 Fourth Street, East Moline, Illinois 61244, Tel. (309) 755-2858

BISHOP HILL HERITAGE SOCIETY 103 N. Bishop Street, Bishop Hill, Illinois 61419-0092, Tel. (309) 927-3899

DELAWARE SWEDISH COLONIAL SOCIETY 606 Church Street, Wilmington, Delaware 19801

NATIONAL COUNCIL OF THE SWEDISH CULTURAL SOCIETY IN AMERICA P.O. Box 802, St. Paul, Minnesota 55108, Tel . (612) 645-8578

NEW SWEDEN IOWA DESCENDANTS 3623 N. 37th Street Arlington, Virginia 22207-4821, Tel. (703) 276-8236

SCANDINAVIAN GENEALOGICAL SOCIETY OF OREGON 1123 7th Street N.W., Salem, Oregon 97304

SEATTLE GENEALOGICAL SOCIETY 8511 15th Ave. N.E., Seattle, Washington 98111, Tel. (206) 522-8658

SWEDISH GENEALOGY PAGES Email:floyd@algonet.se Website ---- http://www. Algonet.se/-floyd/scandgen/

SWEDISH HISTORICAL SOCIETY 404 South 3rd Street, Rockford, Illinois 61104, Tel. (815) 963-5559

UNIVERSITY OF WASHINGTON LIBRARY Manuscripts and University Archives, Box 352900, Seattle, Washington 98195, Tel. (206) 543-1760, Fax (206) 685-8723, Website --- http://www.lib.washington.edu

VASA ORDER OF AMERICAN NATIONAL ARCHIVES 109 S. Main Street, Bishop Hill, Illinois 61419, Tel. (309) 927-3898

REGIONAL LIBRARIES WITH SWEDISH AMERICAN FAMILY RECORDS:

CHICAGO PUBLIC LIBRARY 400 S. State St. Chicago, Illinois 60605, Tel. (312) 747-4999, Fax (312) 747-4962, Website http://www.cpl/lib.uic.edu

FENTON HISTORICAL SOCIETY 67 Washington St., Jamestown, New York 14701, Tel. (716) 664-6256, Fax (716) 483-7524

ILLINOIS STATE HISTORICAL SOCIETY Old State Capital, Springfield, Illinois 62701, Tel. (217) 524-7216, Fax (217) 785-6250, Website --- http://www.state.ill.us/

MINNESOTA HISTORICAL SOCIETY 690 Cedar St., St. Paul, Minnesota 55101, Website --- http://www.mn.hs.org

NEBRASKA STATE HISTORICAL SOCIETY 1500 R Street, Omaha, Nebraska 68501, Tel. (402) 471-4751, Fax (402) 471-3100

NEW SWEDEN HISTORICAL SOCIETY New Sweden, Maine 04762

NEW YORK PUBLIC LIBRARY 5th Ave. & 42nd Street, New York, New York 10018, Tel. (212) 930-0800, Fax (212) 921-2546, Website --- http://www.nypl.org

ROCK ISLAND PUBLIC LIBRARY 401 19th St., Rock Island, Illinois 61201, Tel. (309) 788-7627, Fax (309) 788-6391

ROCKFORD PUBLIC LIBRARY 215 N. Wyman, Rockford, Illinois 61101, Tel. (815) 965-6731, Fax 9815) 965-0866

GENERAL SCANDINAVIAN RESOURCES

While the majority of national genealogical repositories, historical societies, and local libraries possess documents detailing the American experience of only one specific ethnic group, there are several agencies which are both national in scope and pan-Scandinavian in focus.

The following pages identify resources to which the genealogical researcher can turn in confidence that he or she will discover information relating to the immigration and settlement of people from all five Nordic countries.

Flags of the five Nordic Countries

THE NORDIC HERITAGE MUSEUM
3014 N.W. 67th Street
Seattle, Washington 98117
Tel. (206) 789-5707

This museum has family and church historical records on all five of the Scandinavian groups. It opened in 1980 using a 1907 red-brick school house in the predominantly Scandinavian Ballard section of Seattle.
In addition to historical records a special feature of the museum is rooms dedicated to the traditions of each group featuring artifacts, tools, and industrial equipment related to the various trades and occupations of people from Scandinavia.

The museum has a library with 12,000 volumes for assisting those doing research as well as language schools which are held periodically.

SCANDINAVIAN AMERICAN GENEALOGICAL SOCIETY
P.O. Box 16069
St. Paul, Minnesota 55116-0069

This group is a cooperating branch of the Minnesota Genealogical Society which also has sections of other ethnic groups. The five Nordic subgroups meet independently on a periodic basis. Each of these group meetings is designed to serve as a forum with the purpose of assisting members in developing research methods, discovering new historical sources, and in updating additional municipality and library records.

TRINITY EVANGELICAL DIVINITY SCHOOL
Rolfing Library
2065 Half Day Road
Deerfield, Illinois 60015
Tel. (708) 945-8800, Fax (708) 317-8090

This institution was founded by the Evangelical Free Church which is a merger of the Norwegian-Danish Evangelical Free Church Association and the Swedish Evangelical free Church Association. Thus archival records relating to a number of groups are available.

The school dates back to 1897 and the library contains family records, genealogies, Bibles and hymnals in both English and various Scandinavian languages.

They also have the official archives of the Evangelical Free Church as well as historical documents relating to the history of the college and the divinity school.

SCANDINAVIAN PERIODICALS AND NEWSPAPERS:

At one time in American history there were more than 100 papers being printed by the five Scandinavian communities . However, due to the gradual assimilation into the prevailing culture and succeeding generations of American-born children, the number has dropped dramatically. Many of these papers were of local orientation carrying news of events in a somewhat limited geographical location, although some were national in scope. It is primarily those in the latter category that have survived to this day and continue to serve the interests of the various ethnic communities.

A listing of those which continue to be published today include:

DANISH LANGUAGE

Danske Pioneer 1582 Glen Lake Road, Hoffman Estates, Illinois 60195

American Dane 3717 Harney St., Omaha, Nebraska 68131

Western Viking 2040 N.W. Market St., Seattle, Washington 98107

Modersmaalet Box 306, Oakville, Ontario; Canada L6J 5A2

Scandinavian Canadian Businessman Box 306, Oakville, Ont. L6J 5A2

FINNISH LANGUAGE

American Uutiset Box 8147, Lantana, Florida 33462

Raivaaja P.O. Box 600, Fitchburg, Massachusetts 01420

New Yorkin Uutiset 4422 English Ave., Brooklyn, N.Y. 11220

Aikamme P.O. Box 76979 Vancouver, B.C. Canada V5R 5T3

Canadian Uutiset P.O. Box 2418, Thunder Bay, Ontario Canada P7B 5E9

Vapaa Sana 400 Queen St. W., Toronto, Ontario Canada M5V 2A6

Velseysviesta 11900 SE McGillvary, Vancouver,Washington 98684

Scandinavian Canadian Businessman Box 306, Oakville, Ont. L6J 5A2

ICELANDIC LANGUAGE

Logberg-Helmskringia 525 Kylemore Winnipeg, Manitoba Canada I6J 5A2

NORWEGIAN LANGUAGE

Ny Verd 10085 Suman Circle, Eden Prairie, Minnesota 55344

The Viking 1455 W. Lake, Minneapolis, Minnesota 55408

Nordiske Tidende 8104 5th Ave, Brooklyn, N.Y. 11209

Western Viking 2040 N.W. Market St., Seattle, Washington 98107

Scandinavian Canadian Businessman Box 306, Oakville, Ont. Can L6J5A2

SWEDISH LANGUAGE

Vestkusten 435 Duboce Ave., San Francisco, California 94117

Norden 8104 5th Ave., Brooklyn, New York 11209

Nordstjernan Svea 8104 5th Ave., Brooklyn, New York 11209

Ledstjernan P.O. Box 5182, Vancouver, Washington 98688

Svenska Pressen Box 46800 Stat. G, Vancouver, B.C. V6R 4G6

Scandinavian Canadian Businessman Box 306, Oakville, Ont. L6J 5A2

SCANDINAVIAN STUDIES AND LANGUAGE INSTRUCTION:

There are numerous opportunities nationwide for study of languages and cultures of the five Scandinavian nations. The following section list some of the colleges and universities which offer instructional programs and, in some cases, undergraduate and graduate degrees:

DANISH

Dana College - Blair, Nebraska

Grand View College - Des Moines, Iowa

University of Washington - Seattle, Washington

FINNISH

Finlandia University - Hancock, Michigan

Northern Michigan University - Marquette, Michigan

University of Minnesota - Minneapolis, Minnesota

Indiana University - Bloomington, Indiana

University of Washington - Seattle, Washington

ICELANDIC

University of Washington - Seattle, Washington

University of California - Berkeley, California

University of North Dakota - Grand Forks, North Dakota

NORWEGIAN

St. Olaf College - Northfield, Minnesota

Concordia College - Moorhead, Minnesota

Augustana College - Sioux Falls, South Dakota

Bethany Lutheran College - Mankato, Minnesota

Augsburg College - Minneapolis, Minnesota

Luther College - Decorah, Iowa

Lutheran Brethren Schools- Fergus Falls, Minnesota

University of Minnesota - Minneapolis, Minnesota

University of North Dakota - Grand Forks, North Dakota

Pacific Lutheran University - Tacoma, Washington

University of Washington - Seattle, Washington

University of Wisconsin - Madison, Wisconsin

University of Michigan - Ann Arbor, Michigan

SWEDISH

Augustana College - Rock Island, Illinois

Bethany College - Lindsborg, Kansas

Gustavus Adolphus College - St. Peter, Minnesota

North park College - Chicago, Illinois

Bethel college - St. Paul, Minnesota

University of Pennsylvania - Philadelphia, Pennsylvania

University of Washington - Seattle, Washington

University of Michigan - Ann Arbor, Michigan

PLACES WITH SCANDINAVIAN NAMES:

The following is a sampling of names of towns and villages whose names reveal the national background of their original settlers:

DANISH

Solvang, California
Ringsted, Iowa
Dannebrog, Nebraska
Nysted, Nebraska
Danevang, Texas
Denmark, Wisconsin

FINNISH

Kaleva, Michigan
Nisula, Michigan
Finland, Minneota
Toivola, Minnesota

NORWEGIAN

St. Olaf, Iowa
Norway, Iowa

Norway, Kansas
Norway,Maine
Norway, Michigan
Oslo, Minnesota
Arnegard, North Dakota
Norway, Wisconsin

SWEDISH

Swedesburg, Iowa
Lindsborg, Kansas
New Sweden, Maine
Stockholm, Maine
Malmo, Minnesota
Lindstrom, Minnesota
Strandquist, Minnesota
Upsala, Minnesota
Malmo, Nebraska
Swedesboro, New Jersey
Gothenburg, Nebraska
Stomburg, Nebraska

GENERAL GENEALOGICAL RESOURCES

The following is a partial list of agencies having extensive genealogical materials, including Scandinavian histories, but not limited to them.

AMERICAN FAMILY RECORD ASSOCIATION P.O. Box 15505, Kansas City, Missouri 64106. Located in the Mid Continent Library they publish several periodicals and maintain an Interlibrary Loan catalog. They have about 3,000 titles in their circulating collection.

AGLL P.O. 40, Orting, Washington 98360-0040. They have over 250,000 titles on microfilm and microfiche and have facilities for the microfilming of books documents, and newspapers. They publish Heritage Quest bimonthly and Genealogy Bulletin monthly.

CLAYTON LIBRARY CENTER FOR GENEALOGICAL RESEARCH , Houston Public Library, 5300 Caroline, Houston, Texas 77004-6896. Possesses nationwide genealogy collection including federal military service and pensions through the Spanish-American War. They also have county, state, and federal records as well as passenger lists and lineage materials from many patriotic societies.

FAMILY HISTORY LIBRARY OF THE CHURCH OF LATTER DAY SAINTS 35 North West Temple, Salt Lake City, Utah 84150. No individual research services are provided, but local branch libraries throughout the world provide opportunities to obtain microfilm copies of the holding of the Family History Library.

IMMIGRATION AND NATURALIZATION SERVICE Chester Arthur Bldg, 425 I St. N.W. Washington, D.C. 20536. The INS has duplicate records of all naturalizations occurring after Sept. 26, 1906. Requests for information on naturalizations can be made by supplying full name, date, and country of birth, and for arrival records by giving port of entry, date of arrival, and, if possible, the name of the ship.

LIBRARY OF CONGRESS Local History and Genealogy Reading Room, Thomas Jefferson Bldg., 10 First Street, Washington, D.C. 20540. They possess extensive materials relating to genealogies and local histories.

NATIONAL ARCHIVES 7th Street and Pennsylvania Avenue, Washington, D.C. 20408. They conduct workshops on genealogical research and publish numerous books including Guide of Genealogical Research in the National Archives.

NATIONAL GENEALOGICAL SOCIETY 4527 17th Street North, Arlington, Virginia 22207. Publishes the NGS Quarterly and NGS Newsletter bimonthly and has extensive family files as well as a Bible records collection.

BIBLIOGRAPHY

To produce a complete bibliography of all works related to the Scandinavian experience would require a volume in itself. The following list is a selective one designed to stimulate further reading in the various aspects of the subject,

GENERAL WORKS

Almgren, Bertil. *The Vikings Avenal.* NJ; Outlet Books, 1968.
Anderson, Sven. *Viking Enterprise.* New York; AMS Press, 1936.
Bronsted, J. *The Vikings.* New York: Viking Press, 1960.
Evjen, J. *The Scandinavian Immigrants in NY.* Minneapolis: Holter, 1916.
Furer, H. *The Scandinavians in America.* Dobbs Ferry: Oceana, 1972.
Gaustad, E.S. *A Religious History of America.* New York: Harper, 1966.
Hansen, M. *The Immigrant in American History.* Cambridge: Harper, 1940.
Hardy, G. *The Norse Discoveries of America.* New York: Oxford, 1921.
Jones, Gwyn. *A History of the Vikings.* New York; Oxford, 1984.
Morrison, S. *The European Discovery of America.* New York: Oxford, 1971.
Nelson, C. *The Lutherans in America.* Philadelphia: Fortress, 1975.
Stephenson, G. *A History of American Immigration.* Boston: Ginn, 1926.
Wahlgren, Erik. *The Vikings and America.* New York: Thames, 1986.
Wentz, A.R. *The Lutheran Church in American History.* Philadelphia: Fortress, 1938.
Wilson, David. *The Vikings and Their Origins.* New York: Thames, 1989.

DANISH

Christensen, T. *The History of the Danes in Iowa.* New York: Arno, 1952.
Christensen, T. *Dansk Amerikansk Histories.* Cedar Falls: Holst, 1927.
Christman, N. *The Danish American.* Saratoga: R&E Research, 1935.
Davis, John. *The Danish Texans.* Austin: University of Texas Press, 1979.
Hansen, T. *That All Good Seed Strike Root.* Des Moines: Grand View, 1996.

Hansen, Thorwald. *Church Divided* . Unpublished.
Jensen, John. *The United Evangelical Lutheran Church*. Minneapolis:
     Augsburg, 1964.
Larson, W. *Danish Americans of Washington*. Seattle: Pioneer, 1889.
Mortensen, E. *The Danish Lutheran Church*. Philadelphia: Ed Publ., 1967.
Mortensen, E. *Danish American Life*. Salem, NH: Arno, 1978.
Nielsen, A. *Life in American Denmark*. Salem, NH: Arno, 1973.
Nielsen, G. *Danish America*. Washington DC: Twayne, 1931.
Nyholm, P. *A Study in Immigration History*. Copenhagen: Inst., 1960.

FINNISH

Engle, Eloise. *The Finns in America*. Minneapolis: Lerner, 1977.
Jalkanen, Ralph. *Finns in North America*.East Lansing, Mich: St. UP,
     1964.
Jalkanen, Ralph. *The Faith of the Finns*. East Lansing, Mich: St. UP , 1972.
Hoglund, A. *Finnish Immigrants in America*. Madison: U of Wisc, 1960.
Holmio, Armas. *The Suomi Synod*. Rock Island: Augustan Bk Concern,
     1940.
Kolehmainen, J. *Finns in America*. New York Teachers College, 1960.
Puotinen, A. *Finnish Radicals and Religion*. Chicago: U Chic. Pr., 1979.
Saarnivaara U. *History of the Laestadian*. Ironwood Natl Publ., 1947.
Wargelin, J. *The Americanization of the Finns*. Hancock: Finn Bk Conc.
     1924.
Wuorinen, J. *Finns on the Delaware*. New York: Columbia, 1938.

ICELANDIC

Gjerste, Knut. *History of Iceland*. New York: Macmillan, 1924.
Hermansson, H. *Northmen in America*. Millwood, NJ: Kraus, 1972.
Hermansson, H. *The Problem of Wineland*. Millwood, NJ: Kraus, 1936.
Magnusson, M. *Vineland Saga*. New York: Thames, 1986.
Olafson, K. *The Icelandic Lutheran Synod*. Unpublished.
Stefansson, V. *The First American Republic*. Westport: Greenwood, 1979.
Walters, T. *Modern Sagas : Icelanders in North America*. Fargo Instit.,
     1953.

NORWEGIAN

Anderson, Arlow.   *The Norwegian Americans*.   Washington, DC:
    Twayne, 1975.
Blegen, T. *Norwegian Migration to America*. Northfield: Nor. His. Assn.,
    1940.
Gjerset, K. *Norwegian Sailors in America*. New York: Arno, 1933.
Hillebrand P. *Norwegians in America*. Minneapolis: Lerner, 1967.
Nelson, E. *Lutheran Church Among Norwegian Americans People*.
    Minneapolis: Augsburg, 1960.
Norlie, O. *History of the Norwegian People*. Brooklyn: Haskell, 1972.
Preuss, J. Norseman. *Found a Church*. Minneapolis: Augsburg, 1953.
Qualey, C. *Norwegian Settlements in the US*. Minneapolis: Augsburg,
    1938.
Rhone, J. *Norwegian American Lutheranism*.   Minneapolis: Augsburg,
    1949.

SWEDISH

Anders, J. *Swedish Methodism in Minnesota*. Chicago: Swedish Bull.,
    1928.
Arden, G. *Augustana Heritage*. Minneapolis: Augsburg, 1963.
Arden, G. *The Journals of Eric Norelius*. Philadelphia: Fortress, 1967.
Backland, J. *Swedish Baptists in America*. Chicago: University of Chicago
    Press, 1933.
Benson, A. *Swedes in America*.   Brooklyn: Haskell, 1973.
Carlson, L. *History of North ParkCollege* . Chicago:Covenant, 1941.
Clay, J. *Annals of Swedes on the Delaware*.   Phila: Amer. Swed., 1914.
Erdahl, S. *The Bishop Hill Colony*. Champaign: Illinois His. Soc., 1925.
Janson, F. *Background of Swedish Immigration*. Salem, NH.: Arno, 1979.
Johnson, A. *Swedish Settlements on the Delaware*. Philadelphia, 1911.
Hakanson , N. *Swedish immigrants in Lincoln's Time*. New York: Harper,
    1942.
Magnuson, N. *How We Grew*. St. Paul: Baptist General, 1978.
Nelson , H. *The Swedes & Swedish Settlements*. Salem NH: Arno, 1979.
Olson, O. *A Century of Life and Growth*. Rock Island: Augustana, 1948.
Olson, O. *The Augustana Lutheran Church*. Rock Island: Augustana, 1950.

Olsson, K. *By Our Spirit*. Chicago: Covenant Press, 1962.

Pihlblad, C. *The Kansas Swedes*. Southwestern Soc. Qtrly, 1931.

Rosenquist, C. *The Swedes of Texas*. Philadelphia: American Swedish Historical Society ,1945.

Strand, A. *A History of Swedish America*. Chicago: University of Chicago Press, 1916.